SUSTAINING THE HEART OF YOUR CHURCH

Twenty Exercises to Help Church Leaders Overcome
Lingering Corporate Dysfunction

By Mark Barnard

September 2015

ISBN-10: 1516965639
ISBN-13: 978-1516965632

DEDICATION

To those courageous local church leaders who have sought to hear
from, and respond to, the Lord of the Church.
May their tribe increase.

TABLE OF CONTENTS

INTRODUCTION

Healing. It's one of the human body's most amazing features. Blood coagulates to slow bleeding. Broken bones knit together. Skin reseals over cuts and scratches. Antibodies attack infections. We take the human body's ability to heal itself as an assured certainty.

But sometimes the body needs outside help. At that point we call in doctors. And after most medical procedures a recovery period follows. Scrapes and cuts prove tender for days after treatment. Broken bones take time to heal, often encumbering us with cast and crutches. It can take months to recover from surgery. In the mean time we hobble around waiting for our bodies to complete their healing work. Much the same could be said of churches that seek to heal painful corporate wounds.

If you've picked up this book, there is a good chance you've read *Healing the Heart of Your Church* by Dr. Kenneth Quick. It may also be that your church *body* has endeavored to apply the principles of corporate healing, found in Dr. Quick's book. You addressed painful issues in the history of your church. You reconciled with injured parties. You sought the Lord's healing of your ministry. As a result there is a high probability that your church enjoys a new spirit.

The good news is that you, as church leaders, have completed some of the hardest work you could ever be called upon to perform. You have tended to the painful history of your church in a way God can bless. Now you look forward to a more fruitful ministry.

But here's the challenging news. There's more work to do. It takes time for some corporate wounds to *fully* heal. If the bones of your church have been reset, you might expect to be less mobile – at least for a while. If major joints have been replaced, your church may have to go through painful therapy to regain your ministry's stride. Some of your recovery will require you, as leaders, to address the health of your church into the future. Part of your church's recovery may require church leaders to get healthier themselves, which is an ongoing process.

How long will recovery take? When can you get on with your ministry plan and leave the past behind? The patience needed to get well may be the reason we call patients, patients! The truth is; your church's prognosis for a return to full-fledged ministry can depend on how well you handle the recovery period. We've learned that just as Jesus was speaking to your church through the painful crises you faced in the past, He continues to speak as your church recovers from those wounds. You must learn to listen to His voice as you endure the therapy He provides.

Jesus knows how long your church operated in dysfunction. He knows your past tendencies toward relational and spiritual anemia. If anyone has an accurate record of your church's spiritual health history it is Him. The recovery period you now face is designed by Jesus to bring you back to full strength. It doesn't take long, *at least not from His perspective.*

This book is designed to help you navigate the recovery period. In the recovery period your church will face tests that challenge you to respond in ways that reflect a new spiritual trajectory. Jesus will give you opportunities to trust Him that may be particularly uncomfortable. At some point He will likely remove your crutches, as you learn to lean on Him alone. Everything you imagine a physical therapist doing to heal a human body, you can anticipate Jesus doing for your church. He is committed to your *full* healing. He wants to restore the radiance your church was intended to display.

More specifically, this book aims to help you reshape the culture of your church. It does so by crystalizing the lessons you learned during the historical review process that your church previously went through. *Sustaining the Heart of Your Church:*

- Gives ideas for incorporating your new aspirations/values into the everyday life of your church.
- Helps you prepare for predictable threats to your church's new found health.
- Explains how to hear from the Lord in an ongoing manner *as a body.*
- Encourages personal growth in your church's leaders.

As much as we at Blessing Point might like to personally guide you through the recovery phase we know that's not always feasible. So, to help you through the recovery process, *Sustaining the Heart of Your Church* presents important leadership exercises that your ministry will need to find its stride again. As church leaders, you are ultimately responsible for the health of the church entrusted to your care (Heb. 13:17). We can't emphasis enough that the continued health of your church rests on how well you navigate the recovery process.

Be assured that just as the Lord led you to healing, He will guide you through the recovery phase as well. He wants to fully restore the radiance of Christ's bride under your care. Our prayer is that you will courageously embrace your role as church leaders, restoring your church to full health.

For the restored radiance of His Bride,

Mark Barnard, President
Blessing Point Ministries
Ephesians 5:27

HOW TO USE THIS BOOK

Our recommendation is that those going through this book not rush the experience. If your leadership team meets monthly, aim for working through one exercise a month. If a particular assignment takes longer than a month, that's fine. The important thing is that you receive the benefit each exercise is designed to provide. Leaders should answer the questions individually before meeting together to discuss their perspectives. Prayerfully consider your individual answers as well as your group discussions. Invite the Lord to guide you as you address the various issues this book raises.

EXERCISE 1

Overcoming Corporate Homeostasis

What does Jesus say to *every* church? His seven letters to the churches in Revelation chapters 2-3 spell it out in one word - *overcome!* Some of the seven churches in Asia Minor faced threats from within, others from without. Jesus called five of the seven to repent, but He called all seven to overcome. Jesus' word for *every* local church is - *overcome*.

Jesus calls your church to *overcome* just as He did the Seven Churches of Asia Minor. The fact that He calls His churches to overcome assumes they have the capacity to overcome, no matter how the odds are stacked against them. The promises He makes to those who overcome assume Jesus values those that do so. He speak of rewards that elevate overcomers amidst their brethren, in the heavenly realm.

Do you believe that God knows your church's particular challenges? Are you farsighted enough to believe that you will be rewarded for overcoming? Overcoming your church's weaknesses may sometimes seem doubtful. You may even be ready to give up or change churches. That would be the exact opposite of overcoming! God's not done with you or your church. He's working now to untie you from your church's painful past.

What exactly are you seeking to overcome? That will vary with each church. It largely depends on what you heard Jesus say to your church during your historical review. We'll work on itemizing those initiatives in a later exercise. However, just as all churches are called to overcome, there is one thing all churches *need* to overcome and it's the focus of this exercise - *homeostasis.*

Homeostasis is the human body's mechanism for maintaining a level of performance to which it has become accustomed. Take dieting for example. Let's say you determine to lose twenty pounds before the Holidays. After much effort, sweat and pain you accomplish your goal. Looking back on the process some weeks you had dramatic losses. Other weeks your body rebelled, refusing to lose a pound. Your body's stubborn refusal to burn fat occurred even when you *increased* your exercise. Why? Your metabolism adjusted to your exertion and began to work against you. When your body's metabolism adjusts to weight loss efforts homeostasis is often at work.

Homeostasis rears its ugly head in the counseling room too. The tendency to return to old relational patterns dies hard. People get used to acting, thinking and relating a certain way – even if those ways are harmful. While a patient may desire emotional wellbeing, they really don't know anything different than what they've known in the past. They become accustomed to abusive relationships, poor self-esteem, or other unhealthy patterns. Instead of breaking the pattern, emotional homeostasis kicks in and anything different, unfamiliar, or even healthy feels threatening. As a result, patients who experience healing sometime regress to unhealthy but familiar relational patterns.

Okay, how does this relate to overcoming the challenges your church faces?

- Recognize that patterns of pain are rooted in your church's history. They have been a part of your "body" for a long time. Your church has become accustomed to them. While unhealthy, your church's ways of relating are *familiar* ways.

2

Familiarity breeds content. Contentedness can be a cover for homeostasis, the gravitational pull toward the familiar yet unhealthy ways of the past.

- Understand that your church's homeostasis reflects a contentedness with *dysfunction*. So, whatever the root problems are in your church, there will be a natural tendency to revert to those ways, particularly under stress. (Regression may occur without your realizing it right away.)
- To overcome homeostasis, you must clearly recognize the negative relational and spiritual patterns your church adopted. Even though you may have repented of them in your reconciliation service you must diligently address them when they resurface. And they *will* resurface.

Overcoming corporate homeostasis is the fulcrum upon which the future of your church rests. Will church leaders blindly return to the very things of which they repented? Or will you hold the line when the church body naturally seeks to return to its previous unhealthy but familiar state?

DISCUSSION

1. Review the promises Jesus made to those who overcome in the Seven Letters to the Churches in Rev. 2-3. What do they suggest about Jesus' perspective on challenges that churches face?

2. Upon whom might responsibility for overcoming fall in the local church? Why?

3. How unified are you as leaders in addressing the issues that threaten to undue the good work you've done? What steps can you take to grow in your unity and commitment to shepherd the flock entrusted to your care?

4. What signs of homeostasis have you witnessed in your church body since your reconciliation service?

5. What intentional steps can you take to address the homeostasis you observe?

EXERCISE 1 - PRAYER

Heavenly Father, you have shown us much over these past months. We have made initial attempts to right the course of our church, but we have more work to do. Would you please grant us the faith we need to trust you through this recovery period? Would you help us not to lag behind or run ahead of you? Lord, we need your help to become the church you envision us to be. Grant that we would have unity of spirit and the determination not to fall back into our old ways. Help us to recognize when it happens. Protect us from the insidiousness of homeostasis and grant that we may be among those who *overcome*.

EXERCISE #2

Tying Up Loose Ends

"Therefore if you are presenting your offering at the altar, and there remember that your brother has something against you, leave your offering there before the altar and go; first be reconciled to your brother, and then come and present your offering" (Matthew 5:23-24).

It's interesting that Jesus values reconciliation over our tithes and offerings. He would rather have us heal broken relationships than accept our money. It appears He sees our relationships with each other as extensions of our relationship with Him. Therefore, He makes the believer's priorities clear. Reconcile with your brother *before* bringing Jesus your offering.

"Tying up loose ends" is how we refer to relationships that still need to be reconciled. You likely sought to reconcile with various individuals prior to your Solemn Assembly. You may have done some of this work during the service itself. Sometimes there is more work to do after your Solemn Assembly. Don't rush through this process. Decide to honor God's word by making every effort to reconcile with those whom your church may have hurt.

Go through your historical timeline and identify the conflicts or crises that need attention. What's left to bring to closure and healing? Prioritize the work that still needs to be done. Discuss possible remedies fitting to individual situations. Evaluate if restitution is appropriate. Maybe a pastor was driven out by not paying him. Perhaps a staff member was unjustly fired. Maybe a minority was not permitted to join your church. Perhaps your church has a poor relationship with the community. You'll have to decide the best course of action in each case.

Beyond individual cases of offense there may be *factions* that suffered relational damage. You may need to mediate between groups to facilitate reconciliation. Don't overlook these situations. If ignored they carry the potential to undermine your work down the road.

An apology and satisfying an injustice are not the same. Review the Gibeonites' behavior in 2 Samuel 21. Go the extra mile to settle accounts with individuals and groups who bore the brunt of corporate pain. They may say they don't want you to do anything for them. But you want their blessing on your ministry. Don't settle for receiving the forgiveness of those you treated unjustly. Get the last word on restoring the relationship by rectifying the situation in a substantive manner, one that honors the Lord. Remember, Jesus values restoring peace more than the pieces of money you give to Him.

In some cases you may be unable to reconcile with certain individuals or groups. They might be unwilling to reconcile with you. Or, they may not want to bring up past pain. If nothing else you must deal with the sin on your side of the relationship. Confess your part in the conflict to the Lord. He does not hold you accountable for the response of an offended party. However you must seek forgiveness on behalf of previous offending parties or on your own behalf. Make an honest and diligent attempt(s) at restoring fellowship. If you have done so, and the other party proves unresponsive, lay it before the Lord. Ask Him to accept your attempts to make things right. Be willing to reconcile in the future should the offended person or group have a change of heart.

DISCUSSION

1. Review Matthew 5:23-24. Why do you think Jesus said what he does in these verses? What other scriptures can you think of that highlight the value of relationships within the body?

2. What groups or individuals still require *mediation* to settle offenses?

3. Who among the wounded deserve more than an apology to satisfy an injustice? Ask, "What restitution should we give to make up for the pain we caused those unjustly treated?"

4. If our church's reputation tarnished the name of Christ in our community, do we need to apologize to other churches or to the community at large? How will we accomplish this?

EXERCISE 2 - PRAYER

Heavenly Father, we have been blind to the ripple effect of our corporate sin. People have been wounded. Some may have suffered financially because of the way we treated them. Families have been disrupted, your name tarnished. Oh Lord, help us to see these matters from the perspective of the offended. Help us to remedy these offenses in ways that please you and satisfy them. Teach us to value relationships among ourselves above the tithes and offerings we present to you.

EXERCISE 3

One Question You Must Ask

A question sometimes lingers in the air after a church goes through the Healing the Heart of Your Church process. It's a question that no one likes to contemplate, let alone verbalize. As part of healing your church you have returned your church to its rightful Owner. Now you need to seek His face about your church's future. One particular question beckons.

If your church was especially weak when it began this process and your numbers are now fewer still, you need to ask this question. If your church started for reasons that are less than of "good report," as Paul puts it in Philippians 4:8, you should prayerfully consider it. If your church's resources have dwindled to the point of desperation, this question awaits an answer. Even if your church is large and well off, beware of assuming you already know the answer. We ask this question at the beginning of the recovery process because the answer will strengthen you for the rest of the journey. It could also bring your journey to an abrupt halt. Here's the question: *Does the Lord want our church to continue?*

Read that question over a few times. If you acknowledge that Jesus is the Lord of your church, *it belongs to Him.* You, as church leaders, have been entrusted with the stewardship of a body that *belongs* to Jesus. You need to know if He wills for you to continue to meet as a body. He may have led you through the healing process to help you heal your church's painful past and bring closure to the work in a God honoring manner. I know how jarring

11

it must be to consider such a possibility. But we've seen it happen before. Churches with long painful histories find healing, but the Lord directs the leaders to close the church in a final act of faith.

Final acts of faith are not new. Not all the heroes mentioned in Hebrews 11 experienced victorious outcomes, at least from a human perspective. Some suffered great pain and loss, yet they were still commended for their faith. It takes courage to recognize that while believers enjoy the promise of eternal life, churches are not guaranteed the same. So before you go any farther in the recovery/overcoming process you need a clear leading from the Lord to do so.

You need His confirmation to move forward whether your resources are few or many. If He tells you to move forward and your resources are few, He will provide. If He tells you to close and you have significant resources, trust Him and allocate those resources to other ministries. Resources alone are an insufficient measurement of His will for your church. We are all called to live by faith, whether our resources are great or small. The main question remains: *Does Jesus want our church to continue?*

At some point in the Healing the Heart of Your Church process you should have turned your church over to its rightful Lord. That being the case, His is the only opinion that matters when it comes to the future of your church. His opinion on this issue should be the very first item of consideration as you lead your church into the future. If He leads you to continue the ministry, go forward in faith that He will help you. However, if you sense the time has come to close the church, do it the right way.

Closure of a church, should not be done impulsively or without consultation. Prayerfully discuss the situation among church leaders, denominational leaders and your congregation. Seek confirmation. Remember, if the Lord leads you to close your

12

church, you will be doing what's best for those who have called this church home. The Lord has other plans for them. If you keep the doors open when they should be closed, you merely prolong the inevitable and keep your people from finding the place God has in mind for them to serve.

In essence, you need to discern if your church has been in a holding pattern or in hospice care. If you sense the crises your church experienced in its history were signs of Divine discipline to bring your church back in line with Jesus' heart, you may have simply been in a holding pattern – much like the Israelites who kept circling Mount Sinai. However, if your church has been circling the mountain for decades and is on life support, ask Jesus what this means for you as leaders. I'm not saying that weakness is a sign that you should close. However, it begs the question: *Does Jesus want our church to continue?*

Circumstances alone are insufficient to determine the answer to this all important question. Though they may prod us to pursue an answer. Fatigue is an insufficient indicator. Losing key leaders does not mean you should close either. Low offerings are not a trigger for closure. These challenges in and of themselves may drive us to the Lord, but they do not mean it is time to close up shop.

However, you need assurance that Jesus will lead and guide you into the future. That assurance comes with a fresh awareness that He favors the continuation of your ministry. If He says, "Go forward in faith." Go for it, no matter what the situation looks like. If He says "It's time to bring your labors to a close," trust him and close the work in a God honoring manner.

DISCUSSION

1. It might be good if you spent time praying individually about this issue before discussing it together. As you pray on your

own, what do you sense the Lord saying about this question?

2. Are we willing to follow the Lord, no matter which way He leads us?

3. Are you willing to lay your expectations for the future of your church at the feet of Jesus?

4. What signs of confirmation do you see that lead you in one direction or another?

5. Are we making this decision based on circumstantial or practical considerations alone? Come together and explore what leadings you sense as a group?

6. Should the Lord lead you to close the church, consider reading *Legacy Churches* by Stephen Gray and Franklin Dumond. It will help you close your doors in a way that honors the Lord and the good work your church has done.

EXERCISE 3 - PRAYER

Heavenly Father, we are your children and this is *your* church. We acknowledge the Lordship of your Son and His ownership of our congregation. Jesus holds title to this ministry, not us. His expectations for the future matter more than ours. If you should lead us to continue on, grant us the faith to follow you. Should you tell us that we need to close the doors, let us do it with gratitude for the good you have done through this ministry. Lord, we are at your disposal for whatever course of action brings you the most glory.

EXERCISE 4

Where You Are & Where You Are Going

Things can sometimes feel uncertain after you've healed the heart of your church. It's easy to assume that all which follows will be blessing and light. No doubt some of that is true. There will be signs of the Lord's blessing on the work you have done to honor Him by healing your church, but there is more work, important work, to do. Lazarus may have been raised from the dead, but he still needed to be unwrapped from his grave clothes. He needed to breath fresh air again, regain his bearings and get on with his life.

Something similar happens when a church repents. A church may feel as if its ministry was just raised from the dead, and yet some things still need to be removed, reoriented and released. In this section we want to orient your church's leaders as to what they should expect after their church gets healed. Here is what we have learned. Churches go through distinct phases on the path to corporate health.

Phase One – Congregational Pain: (This is where you were.) Churches, and church leaders, usually have a high tolerance for pain. Like many men, they usually wait till they can wait no more before going to see a doctor. Since these churches often have histories of repetitive crises, it usually takes a major blow—a split, a moral failure, someone absconding with funds—to motivate them to seek help. The effects of such corporate pain include a lack of trust for leaders, poor communication, a weak corporate pulse, and a lack of mission fulfillment.

17

Phase Two – Congregational Healing: (This took place during the Healing the Heart of Your Church process.) A church which has a chance to heal will face the fact that their present pain has its roots in deeper unresolved problems. They also discover that Jesus is speaking to them through the corporate pain, usually a message of His discipline over sins and decisions which displeased Him and which the church ignored. Churches which heal take responsibility for their past. They hold a service of reconciliation to make things right with Christ and each other. The impact of such a service breaks the unhealthy patterns and makes right their corporate relationship with Christ. They then enjoy a change in the spirit of the church and see signs of God's blessing on their efforts.

Phase Three – Congregational Overcoming: (This is where you are.) Here the church works to overcome their previous unhealthy ways of relating. When a church's health suffers for decades, it takes a while to grow out of their "old ways." But with Jesus' help the congregation can aspire to establish new ways of relating, and transform the "culture" of the church. Things which may have characterized them in a dysfunctional way start to change. The Lord sometimes presents a church with challenges and tests to help them overcome in this period. The tests may be obstacles to growth or issues which require leaders to act differently than they had before. As they pass these tests the overall health of the church improves.

Phase Four – Congregational Health: (This is where you're going!) This is where the hard work pays off for church leaders who overcome the obstacles they may face in sustaining their church's new found health. Trust for leaders, which had been in short supply, now starts to grow again, and communication is no longer hampered by distrust. The church's corporate pulse grows stronger, and the church begins to see God work in their midst in new ways.

The truth is, churches can derail this process several ways. First, they may not seek outside help in the first place, leaving their church to repeat the cycles of pain from the past. Second, they may discern their negative patterns and hear the Lord speak to them about issues they need to address but refuse to do so (We've seen it happen more than once.). Third, they can be derailed through regression to old patterns. Having repented and stated they want to change, they fall back into old patterns of behavior. They mimic the Israelites who, facing the challenges of a desert expedition, decided they preferred Egypt for their leeks, onions, and melons. But for churches that resist the magnetism of their "old ways," listening to and following the true Head of their church, a healthier future awaits.

DISCUSSION

1. What strikes you about the four phases of increased congregational health as they relate to your church?

2. How do you see God's hand behind the phases as they are laid out?

3. Do you see these four phases as encouraging or not? Why?

4. What dangers do you sense that threaten to keep you from getting to the last phase?

5. How do the four phases help to set your expectations as church leaders?

EXERCISE 4 – PRAYER

Sovereign Lord, thank you that you walk with us as we travel along this road of healing and recovery. Help us to recognize your presence. Please grant us the strength we need for we are emotionally and physically drained by the path of healing. Sustain us and strengthen our spirits. Grant answers to prayer that we might recognize your favor on our progress. Give us the grace to finish the course laid out before us. May you find this church to be a fragrant offering on that day when our works are examined by You.

EXERCISE 5

Developing your Corporate Covenant

As part of your historical review process you took a factual look at your church's past. You broke your church's history down into three or four segments that made sense to you. You reviewed each era. You noted the blessings your church enjoyed, the things Christ would commend about your ministry. You reflected on the unique challenges you faced, things you overcame as a church body. Additionally you reviewed the crises in your church's history and sought to hear what the Lord would critique about your congregation.

If you have not done so already, review those notes. It is likely that someone has reduced them to type instead of the handwritten notes with which you began. As you review the eras of your church's history, what negative themes or patterns do you recognize? Was there a pattern of mistreatment of church staff? Did you regularly fail to communicate with your pastors? Does a theme of pride reveal itself? Maybe you see a pattern related to finances or immorality among leadership. Usually these themes and patterns run through a church's history, not just one segment of it.

Itemize the negative themes that you see. Then discuss them one at a time and convert each one to a positive aspiration for the future. This will form the basis of a corporate covenant you use to guide the transformation of your church's culture. If you didn't do this before your Solemn Assembly take the time to do it now.

23

Here's a few examples from one church's corporate covenant:
1. We aspire to be a unified, fully functional, church body for God through clearly defined avenues of communication. (Negative Theme: A lack of open communication and cases of individual offense in the body.)
2. We will demonstrate a commitment to each other that takes precedence over conflict. (Negative Theme: A pattern of people leaving the church when they don't like what's happening, running from conflict.)
3. When the Holy Spirit is leading us into a faith situation we will pursue it. (Negative Theme: A tendency to play it safe, slow reaction to opportunities for growth.)
4. We as church leaders will pursue open, transparent, two way communication in the relationship with our pastor. (Negative Theme: A tendency not to talk about major problems especially in relations to the pastor.)
5. We will protect the integrity of this ministry through mutual accountability as church leaders. (Negative Themes: Un-remedied pastoral sin and weak lay leadership.).

You could add a statement about what you will do if you come up short in one of these areas, such as:
6. If we fail in any of these aspects we will acknowledge it before God and seek reconciliation with God and the Body of Christ. (This acknowledges the possibility of failure as you grow and mature in these commitments and your need for God's grace to fulfill them.)

We're not interested in creating a legalistic standard for your church to follow. We want to follow the biblical example found in Ezra 10 that guided the Israelites into a new era of following the Lord.

Don't treat this document lightly. Once complete it will reflect your new values as a church. These statements will reshape the culture of your church as you commit to hold yourself accountable to their ideals. Another reason not to treat this document lightly is because the Lord will hold you to the commitments you make. We've watched with grief as churches ignored or reneged on their corporate covenant with devastating effects, including church closures.

On a positive note your corporate covenant reflects your highest aspirations to please the Lord as a congregation. You're seeking to honor him in your behavior and attitudes, turning away from the old sinful ways of relating you knew in the past. It represents a breath of fresh air for your ministry.

DISCUSSION

1. Who do we need to involve in this process? Do we need more than our designated leaders involved? How can we include others who also went through the Healing the Heart of Your Church process?

2. What repetitive negative themes do we recognize running through our church's history?

3. How can we reframe each negative pattern into a positive aspiration for the future?

4. What's the best way to present our corporate covenant to the church?

EXERCISE 5 - PRAYER

Father God, you know our history better than we know it ourselves. Please open our eyes to the patterns of behavior that displease you. Help us to articulate our hearts desire to please you in the future and reshape the culture of our local church. We implore you for the grace we need to be faithful to the commitments we make. Give us the faithfulness to judge ourselves rightly in these areas that we might not be judged by you. Thank you Lord for your patience with us in the past. May we recognize where we have gone wrong and embrace a new and better spirit as a church body.

EXERCISE 6

Assimilating Your Corporate Covenant Part 1

You've gone through the Healing the Heart of Your Church retreat; you've developed your corporate covenant and held your reconciliation service. Now what? Along with the sense of release that forgiveness and reconciliation provides, and the fresh experience of God's blessing on your church fellowship, you now must work to integrate the important lessons you heard from Jesus at the retreat deep into the fabric of your church. You want to make sure the things Jesus taught you reshape the culture of your church from what it was to what He wants it to become. It takes time to grow out of old ways of relating and you must focus on keeping your corporate commitments to Him so that everyone can grow together.

If you work to integrate your corporate covenant into the life of your church, and then should happen to experience something that reflects your old ways of relating, you will more easily recognize the error and take corrective steps. Progress in the right direction, not perfection, is the goal. Leadership should work carefully and wisely toward the goal of increasing your church's corporate health. Your covenant commitments should help you down that road.

We never want covenant commitments *to get in the way* of our church's relationship to Jesus or become a form of legalism. Instead your covenant should drive you to Him, making clear your corporate responsibilities in the relationship, and still be challenging enough to call you corporately to greater spiritual growth and

27

development. We will always—always!—need His grace to keep such commitments.

The following strategies are adapted from *Extreme Church Makeover*, by Neil Anderson and Chuck Mylander:

1. If you haven't done so already, plan on explaining the commitments of your corporate covenant at your Solemn Assembly/reconciliation service. This is the best place for leaders to lay out the new course for their church, and it is a fitting conclusion to a service of repentance and reconciliation. Some churches turn their corporate covenant into a plaque or banner and hang it in a prominent location. Other churches invite members to sign the covenant at the reconciliation service and then place it in a location where everyone can see it.

   If you've already held your reconciliation service present your corporate covenant as a follow up to your Solemn Assembly. It will communicate that you, as leaders, continue to pursue the heath of the church. It lets the congregation know that you were serious about following through on your repentance with real life change!

2. Once the reconciliation service or Solemn Assembly is behind you, encourage your leaders and members to focus on the corporate covenant for a period of time, praying about its commitments on a daily basis. This will help to weave the commitments into the heart of the church and create spiritual sensitivity to the key issues in the covenant. Appoint someone to send out email reminders to remember to pray along these lines perhaps with Scriptural devotionals attached.

3. Commit yourselves as leaders to honestly assess your progress and pray through your corporate covenant at each of your leadership meetings until it becomes evident that the covenant commitments are showing up in the life of your church. Be patient, as it may take a number of years for all the painful "ways" of your church to change.

4. Develop specific plans on which to work—teach, preach, make a part of membership classes, etc.—regarding each commitment of your corporate covenant. For instance, if Jesus spoke to your church about needing to return to the early commitments and efforts your church made in reaching its community with the Gospel, then make that a focus of *your* church plans. Involve the people who went through your *Healing the Heart of Your Church* to help in deepening your corporate obedience. Changing a *status quo* is not easy. Developing specific plans to advance each of your covenant statements will fall to the spiritual leaders (lay and pastoral) of the church. It is the responsibility of leaders. Schedule special meetings to discuss, pray and seek divine guidance about how to implement your covenant, moving it from statements on paper to a pattern of corporate behavior.

DISCUSSION

1. What can we do to encourage people to more completely to keep our covenantal commitments?

2. Where is Christ clearly working in our Body right now and how can we build on that as it relates to growing in our corporate commitments?

3. Are there resistant areas, ministries or departments in the church that need further education and integration of our new direction?

4. Honestly, do we see ourselves as advancing or regressing in any area of our corporate covenant and what do we need to do about it?

EXERCISE 6 - PRAYER

Oh Lord, help us as we continue on the pathway you have led us. Make us circumspect as we consider the health of the church body you entrusted to us. Keep us from assuming that all will be well without giving intentional oversight to the recovery process. May your Holy Spirit enable our entire church to reflect your glory as you sanctify us corporately. We need you to make these ideals real in us. We humble ourselves before you and declare our need for your enabling grace.

EXERCISE 7

Assimilating Your Corporate Covenant Part 2

Assimilating your corporate covenant into the life of your church is like vaccinating your church against future infection. We can't overemphasize the importance of making your corporate covenant a part of your church's new DNA. Simply creating a corporate covenant will not ward off future infection. Only your courageous implementation will do that. Here are further ideas and suggestions about how to educate and proliferate the covenant among your membership.

1. Pastors should consider preaching through the commitments of the corporate covenant in a sermon series, called "Buying into the Values." Some of the congregation may not have been present for the reconciliation service or the historical retreat, and this is your opportunity to keep everyone focused on the things Christ said to you and your response to them. You can rehearse the painful issues of the past (as Moses did in Deuteronomy) and lay out a Scripture-based path for your corporate future. Be transparent and share your own struggles to keep each commitment in the covenant. Create an environment where it is safe for others to struggle, as long as we keep working to improve and not give up, give in, or fall back. There may be those in the congregation who still need to clean out some old attitudes and behaviors. Give God the opportunity to work more deeply in the hearts of those who participated in the process and those who have not.

2. In larger churches, discuss having individual ministries or departments integrate aspects of the corporate covenant appropriate to that ministry's sphere of influence. The Apostle Paul said "A little leaven leavens the whole lump" regarding the impact of corporate sin. But we have found that spiritual health can be just as infectious. Weave the elements of your corporate covenant through all the ministries of your church in appropriate ways. Challenge leaders of these ministries to develop ways to communicate and implement aspects of the covenant commitments.

3. Hold people accountable to the covenant commitments as a standard of expected behavior. Again, be grace-based and not law-based in doing this, but guard against any recidivism into old patterns. Christ often allows tests of a church's commitments to be different. He wants to know whether your repentance and commitments are authentic. The tests expose the true nature of your corporate heart and whether you are making progress. Don't be surprised when such tests come and see them instead as opportunities to be and do differently than before. The key question is: Will you handle things differently now?

4. Introduce your corporate covenant and church history into your membership process. A membership class is a great place to set forth your commitments and how you came to them. Tell prospective members the true story of your church and what Christ has taught you through pain. As this will become their covenant as well, they need to understand and buy into it. New people rarely know the history of a church before they join. They come with assumptions that your church will be like others they have known, for good or for bad. Teach them what Jesus taught you and they will learn about the spiritual attitudes that are important to your church and why they are. Sharing your new values gives

potential members a heads-up right from the start, and challenges them to consider if your church is the best place for them.

DISCUSSION

1. Are there any issues we are hesitating to talk about that truly need attention?

2. Are there any fresh, creative or symbolic ways can use to help communicate our new course to the congregation?

3. How can we as leaders do a better job modeling the covenant commitments to which we aspire?

4. Are any individuals struggling with the new commitments and what must be done to bring them along with us?

5. How well are we making sure this is a "grace-focused" effort and not legalistic or fostering elitism which will produce hypocrisy among us?

EXERCISE 7 - PRAYER

Heavenly Father, give us eyes to see our congregation as you see it. Enable us to have corporate spiritual awareness to discern what's happening in our church as a whole. Help us to recognize those who are struggling with the process we have been through. Give us the grace we need to extend grace to those who wrestle with the implications of the changes we seek. Bestow a willingness in our congregation to become healthier individuals and members of your body. We love this church Lord. We ask you to help us model that love before the people you have entrusted to us. Fill us with your Spirit as we help our church make the transformation into a healthy expression of your Bride.

EXERCISE 8

Rebuilding Trust

When a church carries scars from painful crises in its history one of the first things to go is trust for leadership. It could be wounded lay leaders who distrust their pastors. It might be a hurt pastor who refuses to trust lay leaders. It could be a loss of trust between the congregation and lay leaders, or between church staff and the elders. A loss of trust in the church system can take many forms.

You recently sought to treat wounds that caused a resulting loss of trust in your church. You confessed your part as leaders in your church's painful past. You publicly repented for your sins and on behalf of those who preceded you in your role. You laid out a course to avoid making the same mistakes again, by developing a corporate covenant. All these activities, if done with authenticity, re-infuse a measure of trust back into the church's relational system.

This new infusion of trust enables you to lead again. However, you need to build on this endowment of trust by acting and behaving in ways that credits additional amounts of trust in your leadership. The trust you initially receive gives followers enough faith to consider following your lead again. Now, you must build on it asking the Lord to help you faithfully steward the responsibilities entrusted to you.

How do leaders behave in such a way that they add to their perceived trustworthiness? It depends on your church's history. One church's elder board kept no record of minutes for a period of years and session meeting notes, when they were taken, were considered confidential. This was an elder RULED church. It experienced great pain related to a dismissive form of leadership. A measure of trust would be restored as the leaders publicly repented. But how would you advise them to build on this initial investment of trust?

Another church enjoyed exponential growth. They so thrived on the adrenaline of activity that no one paid attention to the sense of entitlement that grew in their midst. The sense of entitlement insulated key leaders from criticism, keeping it at bay. All the while a vile leaven of immorality spread behind the scenes. It eventually came to light. The church did some soul searching and repented of their sin in a Solemn Assembly. A measure of trust was extended to the leadership as a result. But how can they build on this? What would you advise such a church to do to cultivate an atmosphere of trust and confidence in the church's leaders?

One large church repeatedly suffered corporate pain due to the mistreatment of church staff. The pain continued to grow through the years until it exploded in an ugly scene. The church searched its heart and discovered that their mistreatment of Christ's servants offended their Savior. Assuming this church repented and reconciled with staff a measure of trust would be infused into the church system. But what kinds of behaviors and attitudes could cause that trust to blossom and grow? What would you advise such a church?

A church we know of experienced pastoral turnover on an average of every three years – over the course of 100 years! That's a lot of pastors. The congregation's distrust of their pastors flowed from what they perceived as pastoral abandonment. However, their pastors viewed the church as a hard place to minister. You can imagine how the two perspectives played off each other. By God's grace the church recognized its painful pattern and repented as a body. A measure of trust was restored as the church sensed the Lord's forgiveness of them. But how would you advise them to build on their renewed sense of trust?

DISCUSSION

1. Work through the four church scenarios above and discuss your recommendations for each church.

2. Reflect on the unique dynamics of your church's painful past. What are the key areas where trust in leadership requires shoring up?

3. Ask the Lord to show you how to strengthen your relationship with particular people or groups within your church. What specific relationships need extra measures of grace to build trust?

4. How can you cultivate a general atmosphere of trust in your church?

5. What strategic steps do you need to take to demonstrate your trustworthiness for the long haul?

EXERCISES 8 - PRAYER

Dear Lord, you have granted us stewardship of this congregation. We need your help to faithfully fulfill our roles. Grant us unity and trust among ourselves as leaders. May a new spirit of confidence flow between pastor and lay leaders, between lay leaders and the congregation. Give us a consciousness of how our actions inspire or deflate trust among those we serve. Above all grant us an unshakable trust in *you* as we follow your lead. Remove any hindrances to following you with full faith in your love for us.

EXERCISE 9

Cultivating Communication

Communication misfires when the imagined pain of tackling difficult issues appears greater than the benefit of wrestling with them. We don't talk about things we should, hurts and broken relationships. We begin talking about things we shouldn't, suspicion and gossip. The process of helpful communication actually gets reversed in wounded congregations.

If your church was in pain for any length of time you likely experienced the devolution of communication. Hurts went unhealed. Confusion went unclarified. Silence got misinterpreted. Conflicts became overblown. Why? Because unhealed hurts in the history of your church magnified every perceived slight. Your decisions went under the microscope because people no longer trusted your leadership.

A church's leadership tends to close ranks under circumstances like these. Normal channels of communication shut down as leaders detach from the rest of the congregation. A bunker mentality may develop allowing less access to decision makers. Undo stress can move leaders to make bad decisions that feel like dictates to those responsible for their implementation. Exasperation results.

Hopefully communication misfires are in the rear view mirror of your ministry now. The anxiety level in your church, which tends to magnify or misconstrue communication, lessens in the light of repentance and reconciliation. However reflection needs to take place about how to lubricate the wheels of communication in your increasingly healthy church.

Evaluation of your church's communication processes will reflect your unique situation. If leaders tended to isolate themselves, you'll have to find a way to reverse that. What can be done to give your leaders a more public face? If your church failed to resolve interpersonal conflict, how will you facilitate biblical conflict resolution? If your church was less than upfront about problems within the body, how will you promote transparency? If your church allowed gossip to run wild like a brush fire, how will you curtail it now? If church discipline previously resulted in more harm than good, how can better communication help? If financial improprieties were a part of your church's history, how can you keep the congregation abreast of the church's financial situation? How will you keep the entire body in the loop on key issues?

One benefit of improved communication will be an increase in trust for the leadership. As you become available to the congregation, resolve conflict in the congregation and demonstrate transparency with the congregation, trust grows. You need that trust. It's the foundation of your future leadership.

If you're going to err in the area of communication, err on the side of transparency. Of course there are some issues that will be on a need to know basis, such as church discipline issues. But be available and open to individuals who come to you with concerns. While you may not be free to discuss the details of disciplinary action, you can lay out the steps you've taken. Be as transparent as you can be. Your followers will understand there are some limits to what you can share. They will respect you for it too!

DISCUSSION

1. Where do we think we are strong in communication and where are we weak?

2. What barriers to communication currently exist and what do we need to do about them?

3. How can leaders be better informed about conflict that needs to be resolved?

4. Are there any issues which we know currently exist which we've chosen to ignore?

5. In what areas of church life would it be helpful to demonstrate increased transparency in our communications?

6. How can our leaders be more available to the congregation?

7. What means of communication must we implement to counter our historic tendencies toward isolation or secrecy?

8. What is the congregation's perception of the leadership's transparency? If lacking, what can we do to change?

EXERCISE 9 - PRAYER

Heavenly Father, give us the courage to risk communicating more openly with our church. Keep us from isolating ourselves from those you have given us to love and disciple. Guard us from falling into any mentality that limits open channels of communication. Give us the wisdom we need to connect the various parts of our body through healthy communication. Fill us with your Spirit as we become more transparent in our relationship with our congregation.

EXERCISE 10

Time Out

No one likes to wait. However in some cases the recovery phase of corporate healing feels like a long pause, where nothing significant is happening. There were initial signs of God's blessing on your repentance, but now things have perhaps grown quiet. When this happens it's not uncommon to begin to wonder what's going on. You feel as if you dealt with your church's past. Should you not now experience ongoing supernatural blessing on your ministry? Why does it seem as if nothing is happening and what does it mean?

A church's ministry is more than what its people do. It's also about what the Lord wants to do among His people. So perhaps, instead of asking why nothing is happening, we should ask; what is God trying to do *in us* during this pause in activity?

While we've seen it before we can only speculate about what God is doing here. We suspect that God causes the pause in activity, direction, or progress to create a buffer between the church's past ministry and its future. In its pre-healed state your church took on a certain spirit which marked its ministry. It could have been a spirit of hyper activity, always reaching for the next exciting event. It could have been a spirit of rebellion, alienating one leader after another. It might have been a spirit of entitlement among church leaders. It could have been a spirit of passivity, as leaders rarely stepped out in faith. Whatever spirit marked the former character of your church, you have sought to repent of it. God wants to wean you from your old ways, which means things must be different going forward.

You want things to be different too! And while you, as church leaders, work to change the culture of your church, the Lord works at it too. The ministry "time out" you sense may be part of His work to help shift the spirit of the church away from what it was known for in the past. The euphoria of healing may pass. When it does God is still at work. He wants to prepare you for the long haul and that may require a period of waiting.

Waiting also seems designed to compel leaders to release their expectations for the church's future. The church's ministry may not continue at the same pace it knew in the past (at least for now). We surmise that this change of pace serves to reorient the leadership. It seems the Lord wants the leaders to lay *everything* about the church at His feet, even its future.

To encourage this, the Lord orchestrates unexpected leadership transitions. He moves key lay leaders on, sometimes even pastors. The reasons these leaders leave the church are sometimes due to fatigue, but at other times they are clearly providential – a new job, retirement, or an unmistakable sense that the Lord is moving one on. From a practical perspective these transitions seem to weaken the church. From a spiritual perspective they may serve to force remaining leaders to depend upon and listen more closely to the Lord during this phase. They may also serve to shift the focus of the church away from key leaders and onto Jesus Himself.

During this "time out" pay attention to the *personal* work God wants to do in your church's leaders. This period of uncertainty may serve to unite church leaders as they look past their need to be busy, desire to act on pragmatics, or whatever former unhealthy mannerism marked them. Jesus wants to be their Head! This period of waiting can be agonizing, but it unbinds personal agendas and unifies your leaders around the Lord's leading alone.

Don't be surprised if some in the congregation grow impatient with how slow things seem to be going. As leaders, you may recognize what the Lord is doing by slowing the ministry of the church. Members don't always have your perspective. They only sense that the pace of ministry has somehow changed. The change feels different to them and they may interpret it as negative or unspiritual. Wait on the Lord even if you get negative feedback. Let Jesus lead your ministry. Listen for His voice. When He senses the time is right, the Lord will reanimate your ministry. In the meantime – *wait* on the Lord.

DISCUSSION

1. What biblical examples of waiting can you think of? How did God's people respond and what was the result?

2. How might God be sifting you as individual leaders during this time? What are you learning about yourself?

3. How can you strengthen your unity as leaders during this slower period of ministry?

4. What can you be doing now to strengthen your church that would be harder to do once the pace of ministry picks up?

5. Have you, as leaders, released your personal agendas and expectations for the future of the church? Of what do you need to let go?

EXERCISE 10 - PRAYER

Heavenly Father, give us the grace to trust you when it seems nothing is happening. We yield our hearts to your examination as we wait on you. Heal us. Purify our motives for ministry. Wean us from the spirit we knew in the past. Unify us as we serve you together. Lord, we lay the future of this church before you. We pray you would be pleased to use us for your glory. We wait on you oh Lord.

EXERCISE 11

Tests Will Come

"And you shall remember all the way which the LORD your God has led you in the wilderness these forty years, that He might humble you, testing you to know what was in your heart, whether you would keep His commandments or not" (Deuteronomy 8:2).

After the Israelites' deliverance from Egypt they embarked on a wilderness journey that lasted *forty* years.   God made no apologies for their wilderness trials. In fact, the reasons He kept them in the wilderness are recorded in Deuteronomy 8:2.   He wanted to humble them and test them. What was His purpose in testing them? He wanted to know what was in their heart. We're they willing to trust Him completely, or, would they return to their old ways?

You don't have to be a seminary educated theologian to recognize that God already knew what resided in their heart. The Lord knew what was going on in Sodom too. But, He still made a personal visit to see for Himself. So we must conclude the Israelites faced tests that would confirm what the Lord already knew. The true condition of their heart would emerge in their response to the tests. Not only would He know their heart's true condition, but if His people paid attention they too would discover who they really were.

We should not be surprised if God does the same thing to a church that repents. One sign that a church is in the overcoming phase is that signs of initial blessing are followed by unexpected challenges.

We have come to call these challenges "tests." The tests often reflect the same kind of crises the church faced in its history, prior to its healing.

Such tests seem designed for two purposes: First, to reveal if the church's corporate repentance was authentic or not. Should a church handle a subsequent "test" in the same dysfunctional manner it displayed before its repentance, it may reveal the superficiality of their repentance.

If repentance proves inauthentic, we postulate that further episodes of pain will follow as signs of the Lord's discipline on the church. The church has not dealt with the root of what they heard Jesus say to them in the earlier phase. We have seen such regression result in church closures, when the true state of a church's heart proves hardened to the Spirit.

Second, tests subsequent to corporate repentance give a church the opportunity to respond in a way that is more in line with the new values to which it aspires. It is as if the Lord is retraining the church to respond to conflict with a new spirit. As a church passes one test, other tests may come. During this phase the church is still weak and may become weaker still, but ultimately if they deal with their tests in a healthy way, they will get stronger. God's intention seems to be to use these tests as opportunities to overcome their old, dysfunctional, ways of relating.

So, consider this a heads up. Your church *will* be tested. The Lord wants to see what's in your corporate heart. He wants you to see it too. Should you be tested, our prayer is that your church behaves in a way consistent with the new spirit God granted to you. However, should your church face a test and you go back to your old ways – *repent afresh before the Lord.* Jesus wants you to grow out of your old ways. The tests that come to your church, after you address your history, help mature your leaders in ways few other experiences can. As long as you make progress toward the kind of church God wants you to be, you're in good shape. However a pattern of regression will lead you to a place you don't want to be – afflicted by *more* corporate pain.

DISCUSSION

1. Are we conscious of any tests that we recently faced or that we are facing now? If so, what are they?

2. How has our current response to a test compared to how we would have handled it in the past?

3. What can we learn about our heart, as a church, by the way we handled the test?

4. What do you think Jesus is saying to us about the way we handled the test?

5. If we failed the test, what can we learn from it and how do we address it before the Lord?

EXERCISE 11 - PRAYER

Dear Heavenly Father, you know what is in the heart of every church, we cannot hide our secret thoughts from you. May the work you did in the heart of our church prove real. When our time to be tested comes, give us the awareness we need to recognize it as such. Grant us the courage and faithfulness to handle it in a way that reflects who you want us to become. We don't want to go back to who we were before. Help us in our hour of testing to seek your face. May our heart be pleasing in your sight.

EXERCISE 12

Reviving Church Discipline

During the recovery phase new health begins to spread through the church body. The church gets healthier as new attitudes take root. The church's culture takes on an atmosphere of joy as the Spirit moves with greater freedom. Lines of communication begin to open. Trust in leaders grows. You begin to get traction on your missional objectives. You must protect your church's new found spiritual health. One way you protect the health of your church is through church discipline.

The call for church discipline *will* come. Some may be slow to adopt the church's new value system. Be patient. However you may need to lovingly confront those who continue to act in ways that reflect your church's painful past. Some erring individuals won't stick around to benefit from church discipline, once they discover you actually plan to implement it. More teachable folk may respond to discipline and make significant progress in their faith. However neither can happen if you fail to implement biblical church discipline. You, as leaders, must guard, protect and promote the spiritual health of your church. Don't let the fear of man get in the way. You bear accountability to the Lord for the condition of His Bride—your church! (Heb. 13:17)

Episodes of church discipline often take the form of different tests that arise. Some of these tests will involve addressing sin in the body. Will the church behave consistently with its new corporate direction, or will leaders shrink from conflict as they may have in the past? For a church to get healthy it *must* discipline itself. Previously, the lack of church discipline resulted in Divine discipline being executed on your church as a whole, in the form of its many crises. But now you've entered a phase of retraining.

Take your new commitments seriously. Listen to all the spiritual gifts held by those speaking to a given discipline issue and trust them. The gifts will reveal all of God's heart on the issue: His justice, mercy, grace, wisdom, etc. Showing such sensitivity makes it clear to people the strength of your commitment to the health of the body.

It's not our intent to develop a format for exercising church discipline. There are many resources available to help you in this area. A book like *The Peacemaker* by Ken Sande can get you started. Your denomination may already have a process outlined in a manual for its churches to follow. Blow the dust off the cover, find your courage, and do the hard work of leadership. You may be shaking in your shoes, but to fail in this regard is like a soldier leaving his post. You stand guard at the gate of your church. Be careful what you let pass.

DISCUSSION

1. Are we prepared to exercise church discipline when the need arises? If not, what must we do to prepare ahead of time?

2. What course of action we will follow?

3. Are there any issues, right now, that require us to exercise church discipline? What are they?

4. What must we do to begin to implement correctives, if needed?

5. How might our past as a church preclude us from exercising church discipline?

6. Has our church been wounded in the past in a way that might lead the congregation to interpret church discipline as spiritual abuse? How does that impact the way we implement church discipline?

7. How can we educate the congregation about the Bible's teaching on church discipline and how it relates to our church?

8. Do our By-Laws need to be reviewed in order to lay out clear expectations for members and church leaders in regard to church discipline? (You may need this to protect yourself from legal action.)

EXERCISE 12 - PRAYER

Heavenly Father, strengthen our hearts to be the leaders you called us to be. Give us the courage to honor you through church discipline. Bind the enemy from encouraging sinful issues to go unaddressed. Reveal any conflicts of interest or family relationships that hinder the free exercise of biblical church discipline in our church. Guard us from harshness. May we correct your flock with the comforting touch of your love. Keep us from turning a blind eye to issues that displease you and hinder our ministry.

EXERCISE 13

Your Church Will Be Pruned

"Every branch in Me that does not bear fruit, He takes away; and every branch that bears fruit, He prunes it so that it may bear more fruit." (John 15:2)

When a church goes through a corporate healing process, it works hard to address the "root issues" which have hindered its ministry and limited its fruit. They repent of those hindering issues before the Lord: They reconcile with injured parties; they seek to right historic wrongs; they confess to their congregation, their previous leaders and sometimes even their city. Addressing such root issues is necessary for possible future fruitful ministry, but sometimes we find that churches then need a little "pruning" too.

Having done the "root work" don't be surprised if you see Jesus begin to prune your congregation. The question is: How does Jesus "prune" a church? To answer that question we need to review some specific principles related to healthy and unhealthy roots and branches.

Unhealthy churches attract unhealthy "branches." It is a difficult and painful truth, but sometimes dysfunctional churches attract dysfunctional people. Discerning folk will often recognize something is wrong in the spirit of a dysfunctional church when they walk in the door. They visit but don't stay. But unhealthy people may be drawn to the ministry, not for healing but because it "fits" their own dysfunction. Does this "like attracts like" principle take place consciously? Not usually. It's as if our unhealthy relational radar recognizes how well we will graft into a particular sick church. The healing of such a church provides a Divine opportunity for such an unhealthy believer to heal as well, but sometimes they choose not to.

Healthy roots challenge unhealthy "branches." When a church repents and turns away from its past painful patterns of behavior, its "spiritual atmosphere" changes for the better. Unhealthy people who were attracted to your previously dysfunctional congregation sense this change and it makes them uncomfortable. In fact, they may feel increasingly *threatened* by your church's new found health and can begin to act out.

Making the cut. As a church and church's leaders get healthier, it changes the way they address conflict. Most churches will hear Jesus speak to this when they walk through their history and feel His reproof over conflicts in the past not handled in a godly way. Leaders then confess and repent, but they also *learn* not to overlook unhealthy reactions or ungodly attitudes when they arise. This can immediately expose people who previously found the church a haven for acting out their unhealthy attitudes and behaviors. The dysfunctional people must now decide: Will we address our personal pain and work toward healing or stay in our dysfunction? The church leadership feels far more empowered to coach them to make the right choice, and the healthy way to face it if they do not.

Pruning should hurt! Some of these troubled individuals and families may decide that their personal pain is too difficult to face. When this happens, they will likely look to leave your increasingly healthy church, but sometimes by making a stink before they go. First off, it should *never* be the desire of any church leaders to "get rid" of the people Jesus has entrusted to them. And second, if such pruning is necessary, it needs to be *grieved*, not celebrated. Leaders should always prefer to see the Holy Spirit bring healing and pray toward that end. However, in some cases, wounded people may not be ready for healing and Jesus gives them that choice. They move on rather than address their painful past.

Prune with patience. Church leaders need a tremendous amount of patience with the various "branches" of their church, the same patience Jesus exercises with each of us! Be sensitive to personal pain in people's lives that often drives their bad behavior. But realize that you may not win and heal them all; some dear folks will choose to move on. Love them anyway and burn no bridges. They may "come to their senses" sometime in the future and remember how you tried to help them. So trust the Lord if they leave and entrust them into His care as they move out from under your "shepherding umbrella."

You are all being sanctified together. So walk humbly, but walk faithfully as leaders. Realize that Jesus will prune your congregation to increase its fruitfulness, and know all that this may require of you as you become healthier as a church.

DISCUSSION

1. Are we committed to becoming a healthier expression of the Body of Christ, even if it means correcting those who may try to undermine the process? What will this entail?

2. Will we as church leaders model the courage it takes to become healthier ourselves when our personal history gets in the way of our Christian growth? What issues must I face and work through today?

3. How can we facilitate growing *together* as church leaders, becoming increasingly free from the emotional damage caused by living in a sin-cursed world?

4. Have we developed a "referral network" to which to point members whose personal pain is beyond our ability to minister? If, not who will initiate this?

5. How can we communicate love to our flock in such a way that they will know we have their best in mind when correction is required?

EXERCISE 13 - PRAYER

Dear Lord, none of us is perfect. Even the healthiest among us has room to grow. Enable us as leaders to get the healing we may need in our personal lives and families. Give us willing hearts when it comes to facing the personal pain that hinders our relationship with you and with each other. Enable us to demonstrate grace to each other as we seek to overcome our personal pain. Heal us completely!

EXERCISE 14

Learning to Listen to Jesus as Church Leaders: Part 1

Experiencing the Healing the Heart of Your Church process means taking a crash course in corporate discernment. You discovered that Jesus speaks to a church as a corporate whole. You heard him speak through painful events in your church's history. You listened as the Holy Spirit spoke through variously gifted individuals during your historical retreat. The question remains; how can you continue to hear what Jesus is saying to your church, particularly as leaders?

To continue hearing what Jesus is saying to your church there are three things you must avoid:

1. Avoid adopting cultural methods to lead your church. Most sick churches fall into a pragmatic approach to ministry. It's a natural reflex. We take the business principles from our culture and apply them to our leadership at church. This falls short of hearing from Jesus and discerning His will for your church. It also explains the impotency of the Church in an increasingly godless age. Do we really believe that spiritual leadership should be modeled on worldly practices? A business model applied to church leadership fails to connect us to the heart of Jesus. To connect to His heart we must disengage from a productivity, efficiency, performance and organizational orientation.

   Instead, we must learn to listen to the Holy Spirit. Developing spiritual sensitivity as leaders requires that we

71

have the heart of a disciple who listens to his or her master. Isaiah put it this way, "He awakens *Me* morning by morning, He awakens My ear to listen as a disciple" (Isaiah 50:4). While I have no proof, I highly suspect that such a passage motivated our Lord to find lonely places to hear from His heavenly Father about future steps for his earthly ministry. That's the model we should follow, not the latest business guru!

2. Avoid catering to one or two strong voices amongst your church. Catering to those we esteem as "powerful" disfigures the Body of Christ and the way it was intended to operate. It's the practical equivalent of the "eye" saying to the "hand" - "I have no need of you" (1 Cor. 12). When we deem one part of the body so influential that the rest of the body goes ignored, we have a problem. We're after hearing what Jesus is saying to our church - not one or two strong voices within the body. Ask Jesus to give you the backbone to wait on His voice even while lesser voices shout for attention. Listening to the wrong voice is what got humanity into trouble with God in the first place!

3. Avoid clinging to your expectations about the direction of your church. We can't carry an agenda and hope to honestly hear what Jesus wants to say to us. It's His church. We are but stewards. That takes the pressure off *us* as far as charting a path for our church. It also lays responsibility squarely at our feet to be sure that it is His voice we hear. We can't hear his voice if our ears ring with our ideas, wants, preferences and visions. Empty yourselves individually and as a group of leaders of your expectations. Jesus is willing to speak to those who are open to what He has to say. If you're distracted by your agenda, you won't hear His still small voice.

DISCUSSION

1. Of the three practices to avoid, to which one do you feel your church is particularly vulnerable? Why?

2. To what degree is a business model of leadership impacting your leadership of your church?

3. What comfort does following a business model for church leadership provide? What limitations does it contain?

4. Are any strong voices within the body seeking to lead the church in a certain direction? Are you giving too much weight to certain opinions? What do you sense the Holy Spirit saying about that?

5. How willing are you to get alone with God before moving forward with a decision? Individually? As a group of leaders?

6. Are you willing to let go of what you think the church's future looks like? It may require letting go of your agenda *before* God will reveal His.

7. How willing are you to wait for the clear leading of the Lord? This will require you to resist calls for quick action. What problems does this raise?

8. What might be getting in the way of hearing from Jesus about the direction of your church right now? What do you need to do about it?

EXERCISE 14 - PRAYER

Oh Lord, help us to hear your voice. Keep us from being distracted by lesser voices. Protect us from impetuous decisions that lack the confirmation of your peace. Give us unity as leaders in the decisions we make. Grant that, once discerned, no other voice would dissuade us from following you. Give us eyes to see and ears to hear! Enable us to be steadfast leaders who learn to recognize and respond to your voice alone.

EXERCISE 15

Learning to Listen to Jesus as Church Leaders: Part 2

To discern what's on the horizon after your church experiences a measure of healing you must learn to recognize Jesus' voice. As church leaders this is vital to sustaining the health of your church. We've talked about three things to avoid in the previous exercise. Now we want to examine three practices you need to embrace. As you develop your skills in these areas you will abide more closely in the Vine and help your church bear more fruit.

1. Pay attention to pain. Is your church experiencing painful events that mirror the kinds of things you discovered in your church's history? If so, it may indicate that Jesus is still speaking to you about root issues you have failed to address. Go back and take a hard look at the negative patterns in your church's journey. You likely overlooked something Jesus is still trying to bring to your attention. See what you missed. Then deal with it in a biblical, God honoring manner.

   As a result of the Healing the Heart of Your Church process you should have a new degree of corporate spiritual awareness. You will likely not look at painful corporate issues the way you did in the past. If the church is a body and pain comes into that body, the pain is there to speak to you about a problem Jesus sees in the body. Don't settle for what appears like an obvious, practical solution to the pain. Ask Jesus, "What is the real nature of our problem here?" When mixed with faith, He will always answer a prayer like that (James 1:5).

2. Recognize the difference between challenges and crises. Every church faces challenges. You will continue to face them after you church gets healed. A challenge, if mishandled, can become a crisis. If it does you need to discern how to deal with the crisis in a way God can bless. However, if the challenge is simply an obstacle, trial, or setback, that every church faces, ask the Lord how He wants you to overcome it as a body. It is not His discipline of your church. You're simply experiencing the normal kind of difficulties every church must overcome.

    However, difficulties reveal the heart of a people. This comes out clearly in Judges 2:21, "I also will no longer drive out before them any of the nations which Joshua left when he died, in order to test Israel by them, whether they will keep the way of the LORD to walk in it as their fathers did, or not." Jesus may leave difficulties in your midst to reveal what's in your heart as a church, just as God did with the Israelites. The question becomes; how will you handle the challenge when it comes? How you handle the inevitable challenge is key to sustaining the health of your church.

3. Make haste slowly. Discerning what Jesus is saying to your church takes time. If you sense dissonance among the gifts represented by your leaders, you need to slow down. Ask the Lord to make things clear. The urgency to make a decision is not as important as making a decision in line with the Spirit. It's times like this when waiting on the Lord becomes part of discerning the Lord's will. He may be teaching you how to discern his leading through a period of un-clarity. Beware of rushing to settle an issue and missing the opportunity to grow into a group of responsive leaders. Learn to recognize His voice. How much trouble came to

78

biblical characters through impetuous leadership decisions? Learn from the past and stay in step with the Spirit.

DISCUSSION

1. Where are the points of pain in our congregational body? To what might Jesus be drawing our attention through them?

2. If there are points of pain in our body, do they resemble our past episodes of pain? How can we handle our current problems in a way God can bless?

3. If the problems you're facing continue to fester, ask God - "What's the real nature of the problems we're facing?" What do you sense the answer might be?

4. Are the problems we're facing the normal types of challenges all churches face? If so, how does He want us to overcome them?

5. How hard is it for you to slow down and wait for God's leading?

6. What pressures do we feel compelling us to make a particular hasty decision?

7.   What might a premature decision cost you?

EXERCISE 15 - PRAYER

Lord Jesus, this is your church. Help us to stay in step with you. Give us sensitivity to the pain that enters our body. Give us the ability to overcome the challenges we face. May you find the heart of our church to be pleasing in your sight. Help us to recognize what's truly in our heart as a church when tests come. As your stewards of this ministry we acknowledge it is our responsibility to stay in step with you. Give us the patience to wait on you and not stumble through our own impetuousness.

EXERCISE 16

Learning to Listen to Jesus as Church Leaders: Part 3

Listening to Jesus as church leaders is probably the most vital skill you can acquire. We've covered several areas that are important to developing "ears to hear." But there is one approach that bears greater weight than the others. It requires a complete paradigm shift in the way most church leaders approach their roles in the local church. It includes what they hear from the Lord personally but moves on to recognize what Jesus is saying through the rest of the body.

Are you listening to the Holy Spirit speak through the body you serve? Has it ever crossed you mind to do so, or to recognize how Jesus does it? You experienced some of this dynamic during your church's historical review. Now we want to encourage you to continue to have ears to hear as you lead your church into the future.

This approach is based on the biblical assumption that every person in your church body has a spiritual gift. It builds with the idea that Jesus speaks through people with different gifts. Understand that God providentially led particular people to join your church. Those individuals have spiritual gifts that contribute to making your church a fully functional, spiritually sensitive local church body.

We're not talking about embracing a congregational form of government. In fact this approach works whatever form of church government you employ. It has less to do with how people vote and more to do with discerning what Jesus is saying through the variously gifted individuals he has brought to your church. He brought them so your church could fulfill its unique calling in the community where he placed you. Failure to listen to what the Spirit is saying though the various gifts God has given your church is like decapitating the head (leadership, elders, deacons etc.) from the rest of the body.

Our goal is to keep the head and the body together! We don't need to run around like a chicken with its head cut off. Neither do we need to cryogenically preserve the head, as if it's the main thing, at the expense of the body. Neither approach fulfills the biblical model, though many a church operates as if it does.

We know that Jesus gives every believer a spiritual gift, or set of gifts. These gifts serve each believer's unique calling and function in the body of Christ. How does this play out on a practical level? We must recognize the diversity of the gifts and the unity of the Spirit expressed through those gifts. As a result the Holy Spirit sounds different when articulated through people with different gifts. But it's the same Holy Spirt speaking through the different parties. If you have conflict among your leaders it may actually be different gifts perceiving the same situation. What you interpret as opposition may be healthy tension between the gifts in play.

Don't expect one with the gift of administration to view a big financial expenditure the same way one with the gift of faith would. The former might have his foot on the brakes while the latter might put the pedal to the metal! Someone with the gift of mercy will feel very differently about a church discipline issue, say an unmarried pregnant teen in the youth group, than a justice oriented believer with the gift of prophesy. The mercy driven believer seeks to reconcile and heal the situation. The justice driven believer may be focused on seeing evidence of authentic repentance first. Someone with a pastoral gift has a different perspective than a person with the gift of evangelism. One will want to shepherd the flock while the other focuses on seeking new sheep for someone else to shepherd. A person with the gift of leadership may be ready to charge a head with a new strategy. Someone with the gift of wisdom or discernment may sense the timing for a new strategy is not quite right.

Remember the conflict between Paul and Barnabus over whether to take John Mark on the second missionary journey? There are several factors that could have played into that painful conflict. One of the issues was Barnabus' and Paul's differing gifts i.e. the gift of encouragement vs. the gift of apostleship. (Acts 15:36-40). The former would have been far more forgiving of Mark's earlier departure. While the latter would have had a clearer sense of mission and the sacrifice needed to fulfil that mission. His gifting partially explains the tough stance Paul took with John Mark.

You must learn to weigh the gifts among your congregation. Jesus is speaking through all the gifts. It's your job to discern what the tenor of the combined gifts means for your church. This requires those with the gifts of discernment and wisdom to speak up. All the gifts work together to reveal God's design for your ministry. This is the beautiful, multifaceted way Jesus intended the body to operate. It facilitates unity, patience, and love among the body's members. It's a witness to the world of how different people from different backgrounds and races relate to each other in mutual respect and love. Their variety of gifts function together to discern what their true Head is saying to their church. Every member has a role to play as they discern, exercise and grow their gifts.

Don't diminish any gift, even if it's packaged in someone you wouldn't expect to have that gift. All the gifts have something to contribute to what Jesus is saying to your church. Ask God to give you the discernment to recognize what He is saying through the combined gifts he placed in your church.

DISCUSSION

1. Identify and discuss the various gifts held by each person among your leadership. What strengths does this provide your church?

2. Identify the gifts that may be missing among your leaders. How does this influence the future leaders you may want to identify and recruit?

3. What if any gifts are being ignored in your church due to theological, gender, or cultural reasons?

4. How does the decision making process of your church need to change to hear from all the gifts God has placed in your church?

5. How does recognizing healthy tension between seemingly opposing gifts change the way you view conflict?

EXERCISE 16 - PRAYER

Dear Heavenly Father, you have bestowed many gifts among us through the generosity of your Son. Thank you! Forgive us for overlooking certain gifts that have left us handicapped in discerning your voice. Forgive us for falling into conflict instead of recognizing healthy tension between the gifts. Forgive us if we have strayed into pragmatism or impetuousness in decision making. Help us to hear your voice in the midst of ministry. Give us eyes to see and ears to hear what you are saying to us through the variously gifted people you placed in our church.

EXERCISE 17

Invest in the Health of Your Leaders

As a church leader you've done the heavy lifting all through the corporate healing process. You've served your congregation by modeling humility, brokenness and repentance. You addressed tough issues. You've done some of the most difficult work leaders are called upon to perform. It hasn't been easy, but you've done it and you're to be commended for doing so.

Now you're on the right track. Why? Because congregational health starts with leaders and spreads through the church from them. The example you set over the past months is like a breath of fresh air to your congregation.

One of the best things you can do to keep the health flowing is to invest in the emotional and spiritual wellbeing of your leadership. Increasing the health of your leaders equips you to better model healthy leadership. That modeling facilitates greater spiritual health throughout your congregation.

For example; more than one church we've consulted with struggled to respect church staff. These churches typically experience significant corporate pain because they abuse those in support roles. Contrast that with the following scene. A church I attended held a congregational meeting after their morning service to honor the church's administrative assistant. She competently served in her role for 10 years, and in other valuable capacities before that. The elder in charge of personnel issues stood in the pulpit and praised this woman, while she stood at his side. You could tell she would have been happy to disappear into the woodwork. But praise was showered on her anyway as well as a basketful of cards from the congregation expressing gratitude for her service. While she would have been content in the shadows, I thought to myself, *what a way to model how they value staff in this church!*

So the question is; how does a church with a history of pain around staff people become like the one that publicly appreciates them? Something must change in the hearts of the leaders. Something must change that increases the value leaders place on the body's less public but invaluable gifts.

The issue need not be around people in staff related positions. It might be around gender issues. It could be about the abuse of authority. In some cases a history of sexual abuse stains a church. In some churches racial prejudice lingers. Some churches never step out in faith. In any of those scenarios certain heart issues predisposed the leaders to be vulnerable to those types of problems.

Leading your church in a new direction will require personal growth related to your own heart issues. While you likely learned a lot about yourself in the Healing the Heart of Your Church process, there is more to learn. All of us in whatever leadership role we occupy have personal issues to overcome. We carry wounds that need healing. We wrestle with personal hindrances to effectiveness. To model new attitudes we must overcome our old ones, and Jesus is rooting for us to do so.

What's the bottom line? To model healthy attitudes church leaders must *become* healthier. The first step to becoming a healthier church leader is acknowledging your need. Paul wrote to the Corinthians, "For consider your calling, brethren, that there were not many wise according to the flesh, not many mighty, not many noble; but God has chosen the foolish things of the world to shame the wise, and God has chosen the weak things of the world to shame the things which are strong, and the base things of the world and the despised God has chosen" (1 Cor. 1:26-28). None of us come into the Body of Christ with a perfect pedigree. To quote Ken Quick, "We are sinners and sin affects us all very deeply on an emotional level." Emotional damage often goes overlooked in Christian discipleship, but it contributes significantly to congregational dysfunction.

Additionally, if you look at the promises given to those who overcome in Jesus' letters to the churches in Revelation 2-3, all are made to courageous *individuals*. It could easily be inferred that these courageous individuals include church leaders, leaders willing to overcome the personal heart issues that may have facilitated their church's corporate pain.

DISCUSSION

1. How would you describe the personal healing you've already received as part of the Healing the Heart of Your Church process?

2. What areas do you sense that God is challenging you to overcome, personally, as it relates to your leadership in the church?

3. How can you help each other, as leaders, grow into healthier leaders?

4. What resources might you identify and avail yourselves of to accelerate your personal healing/growth?

5. What aspects of your family life have been impacted by the Healing the Heart of Your Church process?

6. What aspects of your family life need further healing?

7. Complete the following sentence. To become a healthier believer and better role model to the congregation, I need to work on: .

8. What actions will you take to address areas where you need personal growth?

EXERCISE 17 - PRAYER

Lord, we need your help to become the leaders you've called us to be. Help us to overcome the personal pain each of us may be carrying. Open our eyes to ways we can become healthier leaders in the church and in our homes. We confess our weakness and need. Lord do a work in us that is evident to our families and congregation. Help us model the kind of spirit you long to see in our church. Strengthen us to overcome our personal issues and those weaknesses that threaten our ministry.

EXERCISE 18

Have Fun as a Church

Weird Al Yankovic, the singer/composer of musical parodies, released an album titled "Mandatory Fun." For churches that need a healthier environment fun should be mandatory! Dysfunctional churches tend to be uptight places. Unresolved conflict elevates the sense of seriousness. A lack of trust for leaders raises the level of congregational anxiety. Undiluted fun has a way of releasing such pressures from the atmosphere.

It's true. You're not necessarily in an overly anxious environment anymore, now that you've sought to resolve your church's corporate pain. Your reconciliation service and subsequent freedom from God's discipline changes the spirit of your church from anxiety to peace.

But there's something about laughter that facilitates positive energy. It communicates that things are going to be alright. It says, "we don't have to take our selves so seriously" (Taking themselves too seriously is often what unhealthy churches do). Laughter helps us let down our guard. Having fun as a congregation is a great way to see each other in a different light. It lubricates relationships and puts people at ease.

Here's a few suggestions. Put together a game night. Set up different stations around your fellowship hall with various board games. Have participants switch tables through the evening. Plan some door prizes or prizes for different categories at the end of the evening. You can involve people of all ages in a game night. One

95

Christian organization I know plays Bunco every year at their Christmas party. 50-60 people, sitting at tables of four, change partners and tables every 5 minutes. It's a blast. At the end of the evening they give out prizes, sing carols and pray together. An idea like that can be applied to any themed occasion.

One church put together an evening called "Taste and Talent." The church's young people put on a show made up of skits, songs, readings, instrumental pieces, and comedy. They even poked mild fun at some of the pastor's foibles. The master of ceremonies told bad jokes. The youth produced a video parody highlighting some aspect of church life. With adult supervision to guide the production a delightful and memorable evening results. Younger kids serve dessert to those in attendance (That's the "taste" part of the evening). Food is always a good idea in a fun environment. It's biblical too. Remember the apostle Paul wrote, "I *buffet* my body." In the Greek that's "buffet" as in "*lunch buffet.*" So there you have it. Come on, lighten up! A little fun may be just what you need to improve the emotional health of your church.

Be sure to invite the whole church even if some don't feel comfortable participating. It takes some people longer than others to allow themselves to relax and let down their guard. In the meantime work with what you have. Intentionally create an atmosphere where you enjoy being together. Enjoying each other's company may be a significant change from what you were used to! I have a sense you'll like the feeling of joy and freedom that comes from being yourself in an atmosphere of "mandatory fun!"

DISCUSSION

1. Where on the calendar can we set apart time to have fun as a church?

2. Who's good at having fun in our church? How can we involve them in planning the event?

3. How can we as leaders model enjoying each other's company?

4. Are there any ways we, as leaders, can promote bonding among ourselves in a fun environment?

5. What hindrances to having fun as a church do we face?

6. How can we overcome any perceived hindrances?

EXERCISE 18 - PRAYER

Heavenly Father, thank you that being uptight is not one of your attributes! Your creation reflects your fun side. How else would we have ended up with the striped zebra, elephants, or, a platypus! Even some of the personalities you have given us reveal your sense of humor. Help us to love our congregation enough to let down our guard, letting them see our fun side. Free us from our uptight natures. Give us creative ideas to facilitate a healthy and anxiety free congregational spirit.

EXERCISE 19

Don't Rush Your Recovery

I don't bounce back like I used to. My aging body takes longer to heal. I sprained my ankle and was shocked at how long it took to return to normal. In my younger days it would have taken much less time to do so. This is a problem with churches too. The recovery phase you've entered can last longer than you think. Yes, your church's relationship with its Lord is healed. Wounded relationships within your congregation may be healed. But the unhealthy ways of relating which you learned before you were healed can take longer to cure.

How long does a church stay in the recovery phase? For some churches the stay is fairly short – perhaps a year or less. Spending shorter time periods in this phase appears to be the case when leaders are growing, spiritually and emotionally. Health spreads from leaders and their spouses to the rest of the congregation. This is an important dynamic that must not be overlooked. The more work leaders allow God to do in them, the quicker the church gets healthy.

The duration of your recovery also depends on how well leaders hold the line on becoming a healthier church body. Are you seeing areas of pain in your congregation that go ignored? Do you implement biblical church discipline when called upon to do so? Have you resisted the temptation to go back to your old patterns of sin and wounding? How well leaders navigate the recovery process impacts how long the church stays in that phase.

In all likelihood the recovery phase will last longer than you think. Why? Jesus sees the true state of your church's heart. He wants to do a thorough job of bringing you to the place of usability for Him. He still walks among the candlesticks as described in the opening chapters of Revelation. He sees the true condition of your church. For your wellbeing and corporate sanctification, He is unwilling to set you on a course of unfettered fruitfulness until he knows that your church can handle it.

The length of time a church spends recovering may also be relative to the depth of the church's previous dysfunction. It's unrealistic to believe that healthy relating will automatically take complete hold if a church suffered from decades of repeated corporate sin or wounding.

Be patient! I know it's hard when everything in our culture pressures us to perform, produce and progress. Our agenda may feel more urgent than the Lord's actually is. Yes, He has things for your church to accomplish. At the same time He wants your church to be healthy enough to sustain the fruit you aspire to produce.

Dysfunction takes time to work itself out of the "body." The impact of your wounds did not occur over night. The relational damage your church suffered likely took place over decades. Should we expect that lingering dysfunction be healed instantly?

Think about the man born blind which Jesus healed in John 9. His physical healing occurred rather quickly. However if you read the passage carefully, there is a *progression* in his understanding of who Jesus was. His enlightenment grew over time. He had much to discover with his new gift of sight. Beyond that his manner of living had to change. What would be his new occupation? How he communicated and related to people no doubt changed as well. The adjustments to his initial healing would take time, but they were good adjustments – meant to improve the quality of his life.

Something similar could be said of the man at the pool of Bethesda who Jesus healed in John 5. He had been lame for 38 years! How did his infirmity shape his life for almost four decades? Were his limitations merely physical? It might be said he had a defeatist attitude, since he complains that others always made it into the healing waters before him. He may have suffered a victim mindset, begging for a living. What shame did he live with as a result of his handicap? What were the cultural stigmas attached to his condition? All these questions contribute to things the man would have to overcome *subsequent* to his physical healing. It's likely that the emotional and relational aspects of his life would take far longer to heal than Jesus' healing of his physical body did.

Is it not the same with each of us? We come to Christ. Our sins get forgiven. We feel set free! However, if we have lived as an unbeliever for any length of time before our salvation, there will be other things in our lives to overcome. It might be emotional damage from our family of origin. It could be that relational damage in our current family needs healing. It could be that our relationship with God needs to be retuned due to poor role models in our family of origin. All this takes *time*.

So while you may be ready to launch into your new future as a forgiven and healed church, let God do what He needs to do in your congregation to make you healthier. He will open doors for you when the time is right. He may open some doors now and other doors later as you continue in healthier ways. Don't look at your church as a project. Look at her as a *patient* who needs time to recover, becoming Jesus' flawless Bride.

Sometimes we have to lay aside our compulsion to *do something* and instead let God do something *in us.* As He makes your church healthier you will recognize open doors when they come. You will also be alert to infections that threaten your church's health. Your picture of what a healthy leader looks like will change too, altering the qualifications you expect of leaders. All this contributes to the overall health of your church. And all this takes time. Remember what the Psalmist said, "Don't be impatient for the Lord to act! Keep traveling steadily along his pathway and in due season he will honor you with every blessing" (Psalm 37:34 TLB).

DISCUSSION

1. What pressures are we facing to produce fruit that may be getting in the way of being ready to bear fruit?

2. Where do we see signs of God's continued work of healing in our congregation?

3. What areas of our corporate covenant need further assimilation into the culture of our church?

4. What lingering issues might the Lord be trying to address among us through recent events?

5. How does the blind man's progression of understanding of who Jesus was in John 9 help us discern what occurs after a church gets healed? How do we see this playing out in our congregation?

6. How does patience play out in our leadership? Are we content to follow the Lord's lead?

7. What do we need to turn over to the Lord that may be prematurely shortening the recovery work our church needs?

EXERCISE 19 – PRAYER

Oh Lord, you know we are impatient people. Our culture drives us to want everything instantly. Yet here we are with a part of your body that needs time to recover from its wounds. Please don't let us miss any ministry opportunities to which we are suited. And please don't let us embark on any projects for which we are not adequately healed. Free us from lingering dysfunction. Give us patience with ourselves and with this congregation. Thank you that in due time you will open doors for us as we travel steadily along your pathway.

EXERCISE 20

Identify and Embrace Your Calling as a Church

Here is the exercise for which you've been waiting! You might have thought it would be the first item of business after your Solemn Assembly, but here it is the last. If you have worked through the nineteen exercises before this one you have taken time to thoroughly heal your church. Well done.

Now you're ready to identify and embrace your unique calling as a church. May the strategy sessions begin! When a church sets out to identify its calling there are four areas that must be clarified; vision, mission, values and ministry model. Of the four you've already done a lot of work on your new *values*. These are reflected in the corporate covenant you put together earlier. It lays out the values to which you aspire in the future. It describes the kind of church you want to be relationally.

Your *vision* describes who God is calling you to be in your community. Your *mission* describes what He wants you to do in your community. Your *ministry model* lays out how you will go about accomplishing your vision and mission. All these components await your study and implementation. As you work to flesh them out remember all you have learned about listening to Jesus corporately, how he speaks through the variously gifted saints He placed in your church. If you listen, rather than purely strategize, you will hear Jesus speak to you about His calling for your church. Don't settle for mere man type stuff. This is not a business you lead. Really seek to hear from the Lord about your place in His plan.

It's likely that your calling will unfold over time. Perhaps important symbols will surface to illustrate your vision. Maybe positive aspects of your church's past ministry will shape your future mission. Your ministry model may emerge when someone with the gift of wisdom articulates a simple plan. Pray, pray and pray some more. Why should God's vision, mission and ministry model for your church be birth only through human reasoning? No, you want God's mind on the matter. Fasting is not out of the question. You're embarking on a new endeavor, one with eternal implications. Make haste prayerfully!

It is at this juncture that we begin to cut apron springs. Our focus has been to get your church healthy enough to bear fruit. How you bear that fruit, and what it looks like, is beyond the scope of this book. Many others feel led to help you define your unique calling and you will find plentiful resources to help you. We entrust you to our loving Lord as you fulfill His purposes in the place where He has planted you. May you be fruitful and multiply. And most importantly may you continue to guard the church entrusted to your care from infection and wounding. We look forward to seeing you among the company of overcomers on that day when our works are presented before the Lord.

DISCUSSION

1. Do we feel that we are ready to pursue God's vision, mission and ministry model for our church? Why or why not?

2. What are we hearing from the Lord as it relates to His vision of who He wants us to be in our community?

3. What are we hearing from the Lord as it relates to His unique mission as a church?

4. Are there clues to what our mission might look like from how God has used us in the past?

5. What are we hearing from the Lord as it relates to a particular ministry model? How does He want us to implement our unique mission? What will it look like in action?

EXERCISE 20 - PRAYER

Heavenly Father, we embark on this next phase of our journey with a great sense of dependence on you. You know our past proclivities. You know our future opportunities. We beseech you to lead us clearly as we set out to fulfill the calling you have for our church in the community where you placed us. Keep us sensitive to your Spirit and the unique ways you speak to churches. We humbly seek your face for the strength we need to overcome the challenges before us. In anticipation of your guidance and blessing we commit to lay all glory for any fruit that may come – *at your feet.*

OTHER RESOURCES TO HELP YOUR CHURCH

Available from churchsmart.com and amazon.com

Healing the Heart of Your Church: How Church Leaders Can Break the Pattern of Historic Corporate Dysfunction, by Dr. Kenneth Quick

Healing the Heart of Your Church Facilitator and Participant Guides, by Mark Barnard and Dr. Kenneth Quick.

Diagnosing the Heart of Your Church: How Church Leaders Can Assess Systemic Corporate Dysfunction, by Mark Barnard

Body Aches: Experiencing and Responding to God's Discipline of Your Church, by Dr. Kenneth Quick

Screwtape's Promotion, by E.H. Muse

The Eighth Letter – Jesus Still Speaks! What is He saying to your church?, by Mark Barnard and Dr. Kenneth Quick

The Path of Revival: Restoring Our Nation One Church at a Time, by Mark Barnard

For more helpful resources visit Blessing Point Ministries - blessingpoint.org

ACKNOWLEDGMENTS

Special thanks to Phil Hagar for challenging me to pursue a follow up component to the Healing the Heart of Your Church process. Thanks also to Tom Bowden whose endless creativity stimulated the idea for a trilogy around Ken Quick's book, *Healing the Heart of Your Church.* And thank you to Ken Quick whose enthusiasm about the idea of a trilogy provided me the motivation to pursue it.

ABOUT THE AUTHOR

Rev. Mark Barnard serves as President of Blessing Point Ministries, which works to heal churches that have been wounded by painful crises. Mark has a BA in Bible and an MA in Pastoral Studies. He authored *The Path of Revival* and *Diagnosing the Heart of Your Church*. He coauthored *The Eighth Letter* as well as the *Healing the Heart of Your Church Facilitator's Guide.* Mark previously served in a variety of pastoral and teaching roles. He, his wife Jeannie, and their children reside in Peachtree City, GA.

DISCUSSION NOTES

55073718R00074

Made in the USA
Charleston, SC
18 April 2016